Lloyd
THE POLICE HC

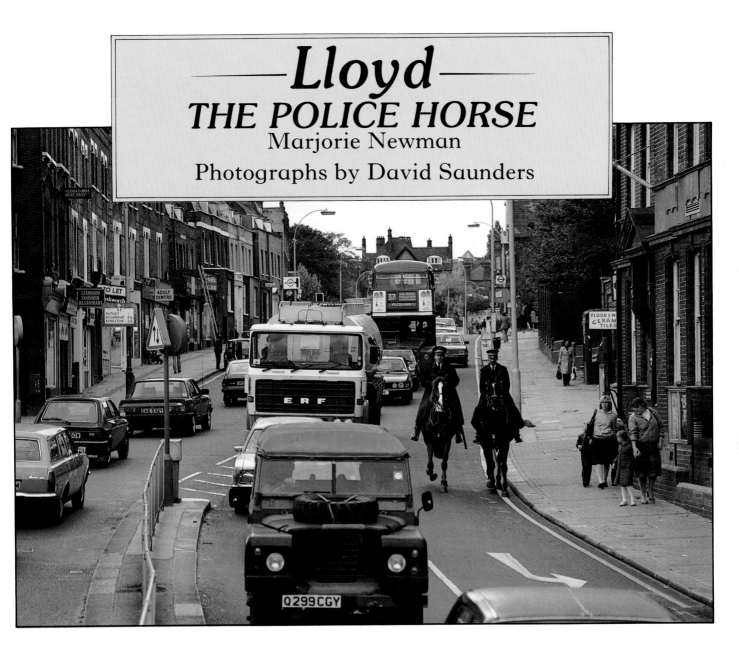

Lloyd
THE POLICE HORSE
Marjorie Newman
Photographs by David Saunders

Hippo Books
Scholastic Publications Limited
London

Scholastic Publications Ltd.,
10 Earlham Street, London WC2H 9RX, UK

Scholastic Inc.,
730 Broadway, New York, NY 10003, USA

Scholastic Tab Publications Ltd.,
123 Newkirk Road, Richmond Hill,
Ontario, L4C 3G5, Canada

Ashton Scholastic Pty. Ltd.,
P O Box 579, Gosford, New South Wales,
Australia

Ashton Scholastic Ltd.,
165 Marua Road, Panmure, Auckland 6,
New Zealand

First published by A & C Black (Publishers) Limited, UK, 1986
under the title *Police Horse*

Published in paperback by Scholastic Publications Ltd., UK, 1988

The author and publishers would like to thank all the members
of the Metropolitan Police who helped to make this book possible.

ISBN 0 590 70790 6

Made and printed by Everbest, Hong Kong

**Other titles available
in this series:
Pang Pon The Elephant
Danny The Guide Dog
Mist The Sheepdog**

This is Lloyd. He is three years old and he has just started training at a school for police horses.

Lloyd travelled to the school in a big police horse box with five other horses.

2

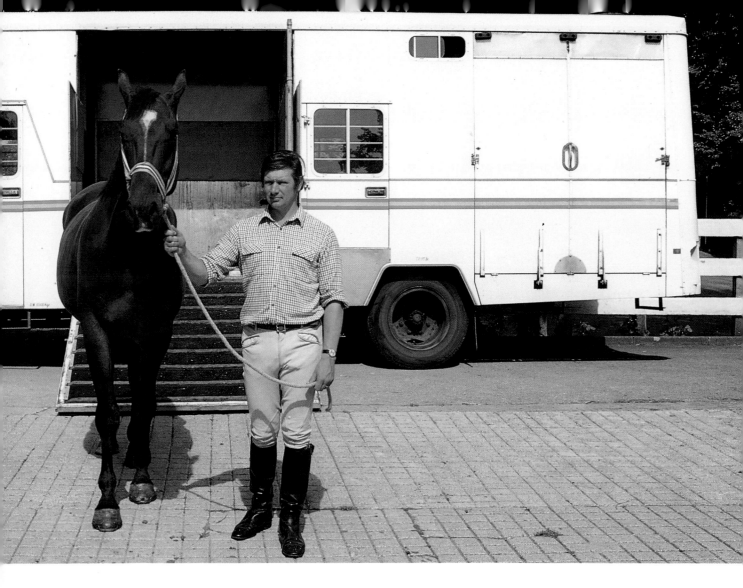

Here he is, coming down the ramp. He feels a bit wobbly after his long journey. Police Constable Seaton is leading him.

PC Seaton will be Lloyd's trainer at the school. He will train Lloyd for about eight months. Then Lloyd will be ready to start work as a police horse.

3

Lloyd is in his loose-box. He can look out and see the other horses and everyone who goes by. There are about fifty four horses at the school. Eighteen of them are young horses, like Lloyd.

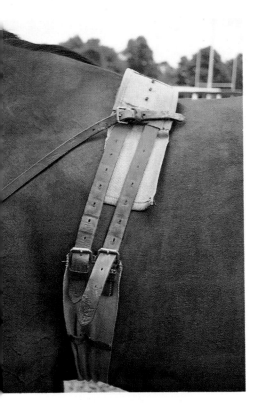

While he's working on the lunge, Lloyd learns to wear a stable-roller. This gets him used to having something round his middle.

It feels very strange to start with. But, by now, Lloyd knows that PC Seaton will never be unkind to him, so he tries to do what PC Seaton wants.

Next, Lloyd gets used to wearing a bridle...

...and a saddle.

Lloyd is getting stronger, but he is still very young. He gets tired quickly. PC Seaton makes sure that the lessons don't go on for too long.

When Lloyd is used to wearing the saddle, he is ready for a very important lesson.

PC Seaton starts by standing in the stirrups for just a few minutes at a time. Then he sits very gently in the saddle. This is called 'backing' a horse.

Lloyd wonders what is happening! Some horses kick and try to get rid of their rider. But Lloyd doesn't make a fuss. PC Seaton is proud of him.

Now when Lloyd works on the lunge, he has
PC Seaton on his back. A helper stands in the
middle of the circle and holds the lunge rein.

PC Seaton tells Lloyd what to do by giving a
gentle pull on the reins or by squeezing with his
legs. Lloyd learns to step sideways, to the right
and to the left. He learns to stand still. He will
need to do all these things when he is a fully
trained police horse.

In between lessons, PC Seaton takes good care of Lloyd. All the police horses are groomed twice a day.

Sometimes they get a shampoo!

After about four months, Lloyd is ready to go outside the school for the first time. An older, fully trained horse goes with him and they keep to quiet roads.

It is very important that Lloyd doesn't get frightened before he is used to the streets. Horses have good memories. If Lloyd is startled by a noisy milk float or even by umbrellas being put up, he will be afraid of them for ever.

Back at the school, PC Seaton shows Lloyd some of the things which might be frightening. Here, Lloyd is learning that flags won't hurt him.

The people who live near the school are kind to the young horses. They don't drive their cars too close, and they understand if a horse treads on their front garden by mistake.

One lady gives mints to the horses when they go past her house. Lloyd's favourites are Extra Strong Mints!

Lloyd's training has to stop for a while. He has flu.

The vet comes to see Lloyd. Here, he is listening to Lloyd's heartbeat with a stethoscope.

Lloyd has special food and plenty of warm straw in his stable. He can lie down and rest. After a month he is well enough to start lessons again.

Lloyd is getting used to busy traffic. He's much fitter now, and rides can last for two or three hours. He needs to wear iron horseshoes to protect his hooves from the hard roads.

Every four weeks, Lloyd's shoes wear out and the farrier comes to fit some new ones. First he heats up the shoes and bangs them into just the right shape for Lloyd's hooves.

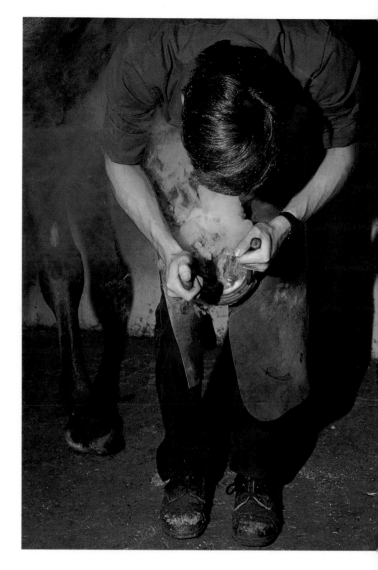

The farrier fixes on the shoes with special nails. This doesn't hurt Lloyd. Horses' hooves are a bit like our toenails. They don't have any feelings. The horseshoe nails turn outwards so that they don't go into the soft part of Lloyd's foot.

Lloyd is nearly ready for his first 'posting'. He is going to work in London. His new rider is called PC Hill.

Before the 'hand-over', PC Hill spends two weeks at the school. He and Lloyd get to know each other. It's very important that they are friends before Lloyd moves to London.

Here are PC Hill and Lloyd on patrol in London.
An older, fully trained police horse goes with
them. At school, Lloyd wore his training kit.
Now that he's on duty, he wears Patrol Dress.

Some children stop to have a look at Lloyd. They
ask his name and want to know how old he is.

Lloyd has to patrol busy streets. The motorists don't know that he's a young horse and they drive much too close. PC Hill keeps up Lloyd's training. He's taking Lloyd to watch the older horses on duty at a football match.

The police horses arrive early and get into their places outside the ground. They help to make sure that the fans for the two football teams go in through different gates. That way, there won't be any fights.

Some of the horses go inside the ground but Lloyd is still in training so he waits outside.

Lloyd will probably be a police horse for fifteen or twenty years. He might do lots of different jobs.

Lloyd might be in the Police Horse Show. He might go on patrol in the streets. If he is 'posted' to Central London, he might be in Trooping the Colour or Changing the Guard. Or he might help to guard the royal coaches.

But, for now, he's still in training. PC Hill says Lloyd still has a lot to learn!

More about police horses

The first police horses. The Police Force has trained and ridden horses for over one hundred years. In 1758, Sir John Fielding started a group of eight 'Peace Officers' to guard against highwaymen. The Peace Officers rode horses and were armed with guns and swords.

By 1805, their numbers had grown and they became known as 'The Bow Street Horse Patrol'. In 1829 they became the first 'mounted section' of the Metropolitan Police. Police women first rode horses in 1971.

Patrol Dress. When on duty a police horse wears 'Patrol Dress' and carries a special wallet on either side of its saddle. Inside the wallets are a first-aid kit, a truncheon, a notebook and pencil, and a flourescent jacket. If a police horse goes on patrol at night, its rider may fix small lamps to the stirrups: a white lamp facing forwards and a red lamp facing backwards.

Feeding. Police horses are working animals, not pets, and they shouldn't normally be given titbits. Police horses are fed three times a day and are also given one third of a bale of hay to last them through the night. Each horse has about 3.0 kg of oats, 1.0 kg of bran and 6.5 kg of hay every day. The young horses are sometimes given cod-liver oil and, in winter, linseed is added to their feed. This helps to build up their weight and make their coats glossy. A horse drinks about 8 gallons of water a day.

Choosing the right horse. Police horses are usually heavyweight hunters. They need to be sturdy and fit as they have a lot of walking to do, and often have to stand for hours at a time. Some police horses also take part in competitions, such as The Horse of the Year Show or the Police Horse Show.

Index

This index will help you to find some of the useful words in the book.